Barbara,
may all
your days be
filled
with Color,
light,
joy + love
May your
spirit XI

Simply
Celebrate

101 Simple Ways to Turn Ordinary Days into an Extraordinary Life

by Sherry Richert Belul
Illustrated by Gregory Bracken

Simply Celebrate
Mad Moon Press • 2005
All rights reserved

Concept/text copyright © 2005 Sherry Richert Belul
Illustrations © 2005 Gregory Dean Bracken

For information, address: Mad Moon Press; 3219 Mission St.,
#3; San Francisco, CA 94110 or call 877-862-1806

Library of Congress Control Number: 2005935842
ISBN 0-9774666-0-4

Manufactured in United States of America

Page 62 quote from Fox in Socks by Dr. Seuss; Published by
Beginner Books, a Division of Random House, Inc. © 1965 by
Theodor Seuss Geisel and Audrey S. Geisel

I've spent my life helping people celebrate incredible, wonderful once-in-a-lifetime events. Not since *The Little Prince* or *The Velveteen Rabbit* have I read such a joyful book that simply celebrates living. I urge you to keep this book near, so that you can pick it up when you are hungry for comfort and your soul needs warmth.

—Robbi Ernst III
Author of *Great Wedding Tips from the Experts* and founder of June Wedding, Inc.

Sherry spots wonderful opportunities where no one else sees them. Her insightful secrets show us how to take delight in moments and rejoice. *Simply Celebrate* reinvigorates the human spirit and moves readers forward with all that is possible in life.

—Romanus Wolter, "The Kick Start Guy"
Entrepreneur magazine's Success Coach,
Author of *Kick Start Your Success* and *Kick Start Your Dream Business*

Gratitude

Kayne Q. Belul for singing songs about cows at the top of his lungs and making me sparkly treasures when I most needed 'em. **Romanus Wolter** for saying, "You can. I'll show you how." **Kirsten Soares** for the lemon pie that fell, her expert editing pen, and all the dreamy things. **Laurie Wagner** for noticing, teaching and being "fearless honesty." **Maya Stein** for lessons in feral living. **Deena Metzger** for the smell of Pine Mountain and for saying, gently, "Not this." **Thea Sullivan** for when it was all "pie in the sky." **Danny Grobani** for the phone calls, chocolate bar, and horoscopes when I was full of doubt. **Amy Blackstone** for her polka dot energy, insightful tea-times at her artist nest, and "Yes!" **Melinda** (and all the monks at the Zen Monastery Practice Center) for saying, over and over, "The voices in your head are not you." **Gordon Mennenga** who suggested we notice even one red shoe on the side of the road. **Suki Haseman** and **Tricia Huebner** for friendship and margaritas like magic elixirs. **Lisa Napoli** for our ribboned braids, John Denver on the porch swing, and everything just as simple and true that came after. **Sue and Norm Kayne** for always lending a hand. **Douglas Anderson** for helping me stand, again and again. **Marilyn Curry**, who'll always be "my writing friend." **My cats** for curling against me, no matter what. **Gigi McElliott** for her contagious laugh and saying, "I know you can." **Cheri Huber** for teaching me, "There is nothing wrong" and how to find Center. **Bob Kayne** for being solid as a rock, patient as Job, and smart as a whip. For his willingness to come running with tech support and good humor, night and day. (And his promise not to tell anyone how crabby and worried I can be.) **Gregory Brad Brick-Bracken** for Saturday Sailin', makin' me laugh, and all the color in this book. My mom, **Becky Richert,** who raised three kids on her own; whose "good morning" notes, nativity set with five assorted wise men, sticky buns, and colorful care packages taught me everything I needed to know about simply celebrating. (And whose letter saying, "It's time. Here's the money," made this book come to life.)
—*Sherry Richert Belul*

It is not necessary, or desirable,
to try to become someone
you think is better than the way you are.

Just be willing to find out
who (how) you really are.

You might be surprised to find
that when you let yourself be
who you really are,
not who you think you are,
or who you're afraid you are,
you really are quite an acceptable person.

And with a little practice
you'll even realize that you are, in fact,
a love-able person.

—Cheri Huber
from *The Key and the Name of the Key is Willingness*

Cheri Huber is a student and teacher in the Soto Zen
tradition. She has devoted 30 years to helping people
free themselves from suffering and enjoy the lives that
are their birthright. She has written 17 books and is host
of a weekly radio show. Cheri is founder and director of
Living Compassion, a nonprofit organization devoted to
bringing peace and compassion to all aspects of life.
www.LivingCompassion.org

Celebrate your favorite color.
Make today "green day" and dress all in
hues of lime and forest. Eat green foods
like broccoli and peas and salad. Savor the
green-ness of nature. And let yourself go
green with envy.

Surprise your boyfriend or girlfriend (or someone you want to be with) with an anonymous invitation to lunch. Find some fancy paper and have someone else write out the invite: Meet me at Ruby's at 12:30 on Thursday. Sign it, "Your secret admirer." To further the fun, be there seated when they arrive …in the darkest glasses and biggest hat you can find!

Some evening when you're all alone, order in your favorite Chinese food. Set out the best china, and find some fresh flowers for the table. Light a few candles and sit yourself down for a delightful dinner for one. Don't forget the linen napkin — can you fold it into the shape of a swan?

Put $5 in an envelope and write on the front "To whomever finds this envelope." Casually leave it somewhere on the sidewalk or under a rock in the park. Have fun providing some abundance for a stranger in the world. Watch how rich you feel after you let go of that money! For extra delight, tie the envelope to a tree branch with a noticeable note: "Who says money doesn't grow on trees?!"

Tell one person today something that you're proud of – that they did or are.

Today, celebrate Mom!
Find a beautiful piece of floral stationery and write at the top, "Ten Things I've Learned From You, Mom." Then make a list of whatever strikes you at the moment. You might tell her how you learned to count to ten before speaking when you were angry ... or maybe how you learned to care for homeless animals. Maybe what you learned was the importance of tradition by baking the Walker Family banana bread every Easter!

Celebrate feeling crabby.
Take a bath and use bubbles. Eat your favorite
foods, even if that means donuts and chocolate
all day. Proclaim "I feel crabby" to everyone—
even the waitress at your coffee shop or the
bag boy at the store. Be real. For added grouchy
fun, be sure to dress all in black, stomp around
a lot and growl "Grrrrr" every chance you get.

Love the one you're with.

Celebrate your roommate, lover, or friend. Announce to her that this is her day. Make signs and hang 'em all over the house. Bake her favorite oatmeal cookies, vacuum her room, or draw her a bath. Ask mutual friends to call and wish her a happy day or send a cheery love note her way. You can even make it anonymous and watch behind-the-scenes with glee!

Sit by the water.

Write, "I love you! You're beautiful" in lipstick on the bathroom mirror for yourself or anyone to see.

Celebrate the unknown. Make a list of all the things you're worried about and things you wish you could control. Light a cranberry candle (or any ole candle!) and burn the list to ashes. Let go of needing to know. Send a note to a friend whom you know is worried about some result. Help him to let go, too.

Buy some of those plastic ice "cubes" in the shape of hearts or whales. Freeze them and use them all the time to give some zip to whatever you're sipping.

Celebrate spiders. Next time you see one in the house take a moment to gently steer her onto a piece of paper and carry her outside. Tell her you'd prefer that she be happy outdoors. And if you're a wee bit afraid of spiders, don't spin a tale about how scary she is ... instead, imagine her in underwear.

Here's something fun to surprise an overnight guest at your house. Save up some trial-size shampoos and soaps from hotels or discount stores. Put them in a little basket, along with a nicely-scripted note that says "For your convenience." Also write a little note that says, "M. Jones, we hope you have a lovely sleep." Put a couple mints on her pillow with this note. If you have a hot pot, you could also put that in her room with a small basket of teas. Most importantly, greet her with a big, so-glad-to-have-you hug.

Overnight guests who have never visited your town will also love it if you place some brochures and a town map in their room, so they can look forward to all the possibilities.

Celebrate your furry companion.
(If you don't have one, how about your
favorite stuffed animal, fish, or friend's
animal?!) Pretend it's his birthday.
Wrap up his favorite treat and let him
open it. Make a little book with some
pictures of him in it and tell your
favorite stories about him—how he
always cuddles in your lap when you're
at the computer. Or the funny swish
of her tail. Wear a party hat and play
some animal tunes like "How much is
that doggie in the window?"

Celebrate tea time.
Grab your favorite mug in the cupboard
and treat yourself to your favorite tea. You
might savor a basic black or delight in an exotic
herbal tea—spiced plum or mango or
blackberry-raspberry. Find a spot in the sun or
curl up in your most comfy armchair if it is gray
out. For added fun next time, go to one of your
local secondhand stores, or rummage around
Grandma's attic to find a beautiful tea cup.
Maybe one with daisies on it or covered in
jewels. If you find two, bring 'em both home.
Next time call a friend and sing "tea for two" to
him. Invite him over for a tea-rifically cozy time.
And don't forget the petit fours!

Hold a baby. Or, next time you pass one on the street, take a moment to stop and connect with a brand-new human, full of sweetness and innocence. This is a good time to remember your own inherent goodness.

Celebrate opening your heart
to abandoned animals.
Volunteer at your local animal shelter.
Cleaning cages or raising money for
creatures in need can make any day into
something special. When you go home at the
end of the day, be sure to give your own Fido

or Fluffy a very
long and loving
hug and
tell 'em they're
doggone great ...
or, um, the cat's
pajamas.

Here's an idea of something special to do for a friend. Pack up a picnic basket (or bucket or grocery bag!) full of her favorite goodies: maybe sparkling juice and chocolate or fresh fruit and bread and cheese. Make sure you bring some fun or fancy glasses and a vase of fresh flowers. A red-checked, striped or spotted cloth and matching (or mis-matched) napkins will add to the fun. Don't tell her where you're taking her. Just tell her to wear her favorite casual clothes. Pick her up with the picnic fun stuff hidden from view. Won't she be delighted when you arrive at a beautiful outdoor spot for a surprise picnic!? Pack some extra punch by lying on your backs in the grass afterward and giggling over cloud shapes slowly floating by.

If it's raining the day of your surprise
picnic, don't despair! An indoor picnic can
be wonderful fun! (And you won't have to
worry about ants in the jam!)

Compliment someone.

Celebrate Tuesdays.
Call some friends and invite them to a
"Totally Tuesday" bash at your place. If it's a
potluck, all the foods must begin with "T." (And
sure, dinner can end with some tasty tea as well!)
Twister, anyone?!

Celebrate your breath.
Set aside ten minutes to sit quietly in a
calm place in your house. Focus on your
breath as much as you can. Breathing
in, breathing out. Watch how it changes,
how it is shallow or deep. Bask in it.

Visit an elderly relative or spend time with
a stranger in a nursing home. Look in her
eyes as she tells you about her children
or the trip she took to Japan decades ago.
Squeeze her hand when you go, and you'll
feel the life-force pulsing between you.

Call off work for half a day and take yourself to
the movies in the afternoon. Wear your
comfiest clothes and don't forget to bring
enough money to treat yourself to the jumbo
bag of popcorn!
If you're not done
with the popcorn by
the time the flick is
over, that calls for a
double feature! (P.S.
Don't tell anyone
where you're going!)

Celebrate the Fred Astaire in you! Turn on the boom box and let yourself dance the night away. Try dancing down the staircase or up on your living room couch! If your feet won't stop bopping, then you could also grab those two-toned shoes (or tennies will do) and check the yellow pages for a dance studio near you that teaches introductory swing dancing. Brave it alone and who knows what the night may bring. Or take your favorite squeeze and two-step 'til the cows come home.

If one of your local
merchants has been
especially helpful,
send him some
homemade cookies or a
handmade card that tells
him how grateful you
are. Or leave a thank-you
message on his machine after hours. It'll have
him beaming all day. And who knows what fun
will be in "store" for him tomorrow!

Throw a Mad-Hatter tea party! Pick up some
assorted teas and frosted animal cookies or
whatever other colorful, goofy treats you see.
Then invite your friends, reminding them that
a hat is a MUST. (Local Goodwills always have a
grand selection of hats… or people can make
their own!) For added delight, have everyone
share a fantastical adventure they'd love to
embark on—with or without the rabbit hole.

Tell someone how you really feel.
Be fearlessly honest, unflinchingly alive,
totally un-tried and true.

Celebrate your sister or a gal pal who treats you like a sis! Take a minute to call her up just to say how much you love her. If you have one, you could make a copy of an old photo of the two of you as kids. Maybe playing on the swing set or standing, hand in hand. For a friend, try digging up the first snapshot you ever took together. How about that one where you're both making silly faces?! Try to remember some of the times she really let you count on her. Now it's easy as 1-2-3 to list what makes her great and send it off.

Skip.

Decoupage! Search through old magazines for pieces of art and words that appeal to you. Invite your friends to do the same and then gather for a decoupage party! Decorate whatever's around the house: an old wooden box, a table, you name it! (Check your local art supply store for materials.)

Celebrate a friendly face in the neighborhood. Think about someone you talk to or pass by every day but whom you don't really know. Leave a note for him at the bus stop or on his porch that says how much he brightens your day.

Wave to a stranger.

Celebrate sleep!
Change the bedding so you have fresh sheets and pillowcases. Before you go to bed, read some poetry or part of an engrossing novel. Try a spritz of your favorite scent on the headboard or dabble a few drops of vanilla from the spice rack onto your pillowcase. If you've got 'em, try a lilac and flax seed eye pillow and some relaxing music. Then allow yourself to curl up snug with no thoughts or worries from the day. Bet you'll be snoozin' before you even think of counting sheep!

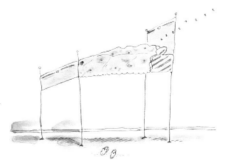

Spice up your life!
Think about when salt was
exotic or when no one in
America had ever tasted
cardamom. Spend a few
minutes in your kitchen,
getting a good whiff of cinnamon or basil.
Get a kick out of the scent of black pepper.
Go to the grocery store and find a spice you've
never used. Buy it, and make a game
of finding a recipe you can use it in!

All the world's a stage!
Pretend you're someone else today.
Wear a costume to the grocery store.
Or just let yourself mask your feelings
if that's what you need.

Celebrate Grandma.
Surprise her with a potted plant or lilac bath beads … just because. Make a list for her of what makes her the best Grandma ever. To tickle her fancy, run an ad in her local paper and share that list with her hometown! She'll feel like a celebrity.

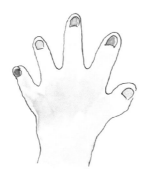

Paint your
nails Day-Glo.

Celebrate splurging.
Give yourself a crisp ten dollar bill and
permission to buy anything splurgy you want!

Maybe it's that metal
bookmark in the
shape of a cat ... or
perhaps that silver
pen that writes so
smoothly. Perhaps
you'll want the giant
banana split or you
might choose that one
huge exotic bloom.
Only one rule: enjoy it immediately—
eat it, slurp it, throw it, sniff it, love it...NOW!

Celebrate the cold.
Fix yourself a steaming mug of hot
chocolate (with tiny marshmallows, of
course!) and build a roaring fire. If you
don't have a fireplace, wrap yourself in
your grandma's handmade quilt and sit
close to the heater! Let yourself just relax,
tasting the chocolate and enjoying being
inside where it is warm.

Celebrate play! Skip to your local
art supply store or discount store and
fill your cart with things that spark
your child-like delight: fluorescent
markers, big chunky crayons, coloring
books, modeling clay, glitter glue! Don't
forget the butcher paper or
construction paper!

Celebrate the next
cycle of the moon.
Look on your
calendar or on the
internet to find out
when the next new
moon is. Take a
candle and write/
carve on it some
question you have or something you wish for.
Every night until the full moon, burn that candle
and focus on what is written on it. On the night
of the full moon, burn the candle down to
nothing and wait for magic to happen!

Celebrate a word, any word! Open the
dictionary and find a word you've never
heard of before or seldom use. Make
sure it's one you particularly like the
sound or the definition of. Something
like sastruga or halcyon or
onomatopoeia. Find as many times
throughout the day that you can slip
this word into conversation. Yikes,
gotta skedaddle before this
confabulation leaves me with
katzenjammer.

Have an adventure in your own backyard!
Take a blanket, a notebook, and a pen and
find a cozy spot in your yard. Give yourself
a time limit—fifteen minutes or half an hour,
and jot down everything you've never no-
ticed before! See the way that leaf looks?
Notice the purple in the center of those tiny
flowers you thought were all white? Look
at the way the willow tree bends down and
nearly touches the ground.

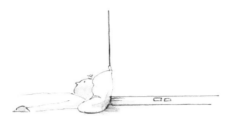

Let yourself be flattened by life. Lie
on the floor. Be very, very gentle
to yourself and trust that you will
stand on your own two feet again.

Take a day trip! Call your local bus
or train station and find a location you
can get to in an hour… someplace
you've never been before. Pack yourself
a lunch and bring along your journal
or favorite book. Enjoy touring around
a new place. Don't forget to stop for a
stretch-penny souvenir!

Celebrate games people play.
Go to your local thrift store or flea market
and hunt for board games. Try to find a game
from your youth: "Yahtzee," "Careers" or
"Battleship." Then rush home to set up a time
to play. Plan a game night with friends and
have fun recalling stories from your childhood
as you dip into fondue. For added delight, have
your friends bring photos of themselves when
they were young. Anyone have the feathered
Farrah Fawcett 'do?!

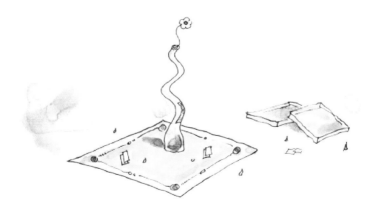

When a friend invites you to lunch, celebrate her kindness by showing up with a bunch of gold and purple helium balloons. To add to her delight, tie a tiny tag on each balloon with a phrase about your friend: "You're a great cook!"… "You always make me laugh!"… "I love the way you look in that red hat!" … she'll be floating on air!

Celebrate the romance of candles.
Buy yourself a handful
of tea lights or
votives. Spend some
extra cents on some
extra SCENTS with
those amazing
aromatherapy candles.

Celebrate the space
between how you
are… and how you
want to be. Feeling a
little like Hyde when
you wanna be kindly
Dr. Jekyll? Take a
moment to consider
that every human being has many different
sides. We're all alternately generous and
selfish, sweet and wicked, peaceful and
upset. Can you find a way to celebrate the
Hyde in you? Maybe it's a good time to chop
some wood, practice karate, or scream really
loudly while you're driving on the freeway.

Put on your favorite red dress today, just for fun. Not going anywhere? Wear it to the market or for a ride on the bus. Or take a walk to your favorite park and relax on a bench, feeling marvelously overdressed ... and overjoyed.

Come to your senses.

Go through your address book
and find a friend whom you
haven't spoken with in ages. Call
'em up out of the blue and
celebrate an old connection. Or
find an old photo of the two of
you and send it off with a little
note and a memory or two.

Dance your joy, grief, sadness,
anger, or fear.

Celebrate someone's return from a trip.
Stand where he can see you at Baggage Claim
with a big sign that says his name and your
"logo"—Bea's Limo Service, at Your Beck and Call.
Hold up the sign and a fresh red rose so he can
see you right when he walks through the door.
Some sparkling fruit juice and plastic glasses in
the car will wow him even more!

Wear many hats.
(Metaphorically, or for real!)

Celebrate your big brother.
Think about something he's really
interested in learning about but
hasn't had the time. Maybe a
particular artist or building a plane?
Buy him a book to support that
interest. Watch his smile grow!

Talk to
an animal.

43

Hug a tree. Smell a flower. Lie down in the snow and make an angel.

Celebrate birds. Think about how magical and marvelous it is that these creatures whisk through the air! Watch how gracefully they soar. Listen to their many different calls and songs. Think about how different it must be for city birds versus country birds. Take some pieces of bread and toss them to your neighborhood feathered friends trilling, "This is for the birds!"

Give someone a pat on the back for something he's accomplished. If he's completed a dreaded project or made a phone call that was really hard, give him some celebration! Maybe take him out for a movie or massage! Ahhhh. Doesn't it feel good to acknowledge something well done (or just something DONE!)?

How about celebrating someone who didn't QUITE accomplish what she wanted, but who tried?! Write a quick email or call to let her know how much her intention and heart really impressed you! Or, send some flowers, bake her muffins, or leave a sign on her door! Winning isn't everything ... but celebrating great attempts sure is!

Don't forget to celebrate your own successes and efforts. Make time to let yourself feel successful. Bask in a bubble bath, take a walk in the sun, or buy yourself bright, beautiful sunflowers to take in the bigness of it all!

Celebrate your newspaper carrier. In the spot where she normally leaves the paper, prop an envelope with her name on it. Inside tuck a five dollar bill or leave a small wrapped package of candy. A gift certificate for a cool drink at the yogurt shop would be great on a hot day.

Let yourself make waves.
Ride a ferry! If there's none near you, then quick,
find the nearest paddle boat rental! Either way,
hop in and enjoy the wind on your face!

Throw a surprise party for
someone—when it isn't her birthday!
Hang signs that say "Happy Lisa!" or
"Way to Go for Being You." It doesn't
have to be fancy—some friends and
pizza will make her day.

Celebrate the weather. Spend a few minutes noticing —really noticing— the clouds in the sky. See the colors behind them and the blue breaks of sky in between. Imagine yourself floating on one. Or curled up in between the downy layers. Feel the air on your face. The hint of rain. Enjoy the changing patterns. If it's snowing or raining, go out and play. And don't forget the yellow rubber boots!

Remember when she . . . .

Celebrate your stories. Spend
some time with a close friend talking
about your favorite childhood memories.
Let yourself laugh over mishaps and smile at
long-forgotten perms and teenage loves.

Celebrate your alter ego. Make
some business cards that say "Sue
Simpson, famous dancer" or "Gino Jones,
dashing daredevil." Next time you're at a
party hand these out with gusto.

Mmmm....peppermint! Take five minutes today to lose yourself in the tingly sweet sensation of a peppermint hard candy, peppermint patty, or even peppermint toothpaste. This astonishing taste is sure to tickle your tongue! If you can't find anything peppermint in your house or office, buy some mint gum at the nearest convenience store. Extra points if you can blow a minty bubble, offer merry mints to an unsuspecting stranger, or find Peppermint Patty in the Peanuts comic strip!

Watch the sunset.

Make a child you know "King (or Queen!) for the Day." Handwrite an invitation to him and plan an outing full of activities to make him feel like royalty! Perhaps an afternoon movie followed by a walk in the park. Or maybe ice-skating at the rink and a fancy dinner out. You could even buy him a paper crown at a party store that he could wear on your outing. For added kicks, give a little drum roll on your thigh whenever she enters the room and loudly proclaim "All rise, here comes the queen!" For your own delight, try tossing some glitter into the commode and tell yourself it's a royal flush!

Celebrate a homeless person on your street or in the city next time you visit. Wrap a $10 bill in a ribbon or buy a fresh bagel and coffee and give it to the first person who asks for help. Maybe stock up on a few gift certificates for local restaurants and hand those out! If you have the willingness, buy yourself a cup of coffee, too, and ask if you can sit down for a while and chat. You may discover surprising parts of yourself through this stranger!

Celebrate the seasons. Buy someone (could be yourself!) a bouquet of spring flowers for the spring equinox. On the summer solstice stay outside until the last rays of light disappear on the longest day of the year. For fall, make a collage of colorful leaves. And celebrate the winter solstice by inviting some friends over for some hot tea and poetry readings about the darkness or snow.

Write neatly on every bill in your
wallet: "May abundance flow
from me to you and back again."

Create a special place for your wildest dreams!
Clear some room on a tabletop or in a corner
of the study. Drape some beautiful gold velvet
material over a box and fill it with symbols of all
you desire. Want to write that play you've had in
your head for years? Then mock up a tiny
booklet with the name of the play on the front.
Or if you're dreaming of a trip to magical

Africa, place a
necklace or photo
from there. Whenever
you pass this special
"altar," give a minute
of thought to what
you'd like to bring
into the world.

All day long today, drink through a crazy straw!

Just finish a terrific book? Celebrate the author by sending him a handwritten note telling him what really moved you about the book. If you're feeling extra celebratory, make a bookmark to show your thanks: cut a rectangular piece of white or colored card stock, cover with a collage of handwritten or computer-generated phrases from his book along with some cut-out pictures from magazines or postcards that represent what the book felt like to you. Guaranteed, your good word will make his day!

Celebrate the creative you! Send
someone a piece of your artwork
or one of your poems. Quick, send
it before you get shy!

Can you listen to the voices
in your head and know that if
they're unkind, they are not
worth listening to?

Buy a package of those tiny,
multi-colored parasols for party foods.
Today, stick one in everything you serve—
even your morning oatmeal! Brighten up
your day...but watch those sharp
toothpicks at the end!

Decorate your kitchen garbage can!
Paint flowers or trees or clouds on it. Let the
kids finger paint their own designs! (And
remember to celebrate the earth by recycling
as much of your garbage as you can!)

Mad? Pummel your pillow.

Celebrate procrastination!
Something on your list to do today that
you reaaally don't want to do? Watch all
the inventive ways you keep yourself from
doing that thing. Enjoy taking a walk or
writing a letter or cleaning the house—just
to avoid the dreaded to-do.

Give yourself two hours at the library. Allow yourself to aimlessly walk the aisles, letting your eyes wander to titles and book shapes that interest you. Pick a subject you have an interest in, find a book, and spend an hour reading in the cozy over-stuffed chair by the window.

Or, go to the library and spend the whole time reading magazines!

Wish upon a star. Now, tell someone what you wished for. Is there one small step you can take toward making it happen?

Leave a note for your mailman: "Thanks for all your hard work! I appreciate the letters and notes you bring my way from far-away friends. Have a great day!!"

Look someone in the eyes when
you're talking to them.

Read a Dr. Seuss book out loud to a child. Or
the child in you. It's hard not to smile when
saying, "Bim and Ben lead bands with brooms.
Ben's band bangs and Bim's band booms."

Pick up a box of bagels, cookies, or
donuts and leave 'em in the lunchroom
with a cheery note that says "Enoy.
Sure hope your day is sweet!!!"

Buy a toy and some ribbon. Make a card that
says "I need a home." Go to the nearest
playground and tie a bow around the toy with
the card attached. Imagine the feeling some
lucky kid will have when he discovers that toy.

Wrap your bicycle handlebars with
multi-colored ribbon!

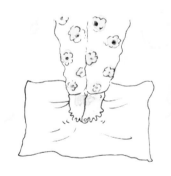

Celebrate your feet!!
Think about how they
hold you up all day
long, for miles on end.
At the end of the day,
soak your feet in warm
water and massage
them gently. Grab
some foot scrub,
creamy lotion, or lavender powder; luxuriate in a
scrub, rub, and puff for those tired tootsies. For
some extra-special pampering, treat those
puppies to a "pet"-icure!

You handled that well. Instead of berating
yourself for all the undone things on your
list, how about giving yourself a pat on
the back for stopping trouble in its tracks,
keeping the balls in the air, or your
fast-track balancing acts.

Celebrate morning.
Do you wake up cranky and bleary-eyed?
Give yourself ten minutes of something
scrumptious to start the day. A dose of yoga?
Fantastic fiction? Perhaps some time to jot
down your dreams and muse about what they
mean? Tomorrow, let yourself wake up and
smell the roses ... and see how sweet it is!

Choose love.
If you're in a fight with someone, mad at
yourself, or angry at the world ... can you
take a deep breath, and allow yourself
just one moment of love? Focus on a child in
your life, a color you delight in, music that
moves you. Redirect your attention to
something—anything—you love.
And feel the lightness it brings,
inside and out.

No matter what you feel, or what has
happened today, can you accept it? Right
now, right here, in this moment, can you
close your eyes and imagine yourself
absolutely at peace? Can you celebrate your
own unique, difficult, raging, grieving,
sweet, cranky, beautiful, unraveling,
uncertain, lovely self? In this one moment,
can you celebrate that you are absolutely
wonderful, exactly as you are?
Celebrate YOU. Unconditionally.

Scribbles, doodles and ponderings on simple celebrations you wish had been in this book:

We want to hear from you!

Did this book inspire you? Did you try any of the celebrations and surprise yourself with the results? We'd love to hear from you!

Will you share any ideas for your own kinds of celebrations with other Simply Celebrate readers?

Go to www.SimplyCelebrate.net to post your ideas! Or, Write to Sherry at the email address below.

Contact Sherry:
Sherry@SimplyCelebrate.net

Contact Gregory:
Gregory@SimplyCelebrate.net